Passive Income

10 Ways to Increase Your Cash Flow

Justin LaCour

Copyright © 2017 Justin LaCour.

All rights reserved. No part of this book may be reproduced, stored, or transmitted by any means—whether auditory, graphic, mechanical, or electronic—without written permission of both publisher and author, except in the case of brief excerpts used in critical articles and reviews. Unauthorized reproduction of any part of this work is illegal and is punishable by law.

I dedicate this book to my wife and kids. You all motivate me to be my best each and every day…

Contents

Chapter 1   The Search for Passive Income 1

Chapter 2   On-line Surveys 3

Chapter 3   EBay 5

Chapter 4   YouTube Channel 9

Chapter 5   Flipping Cars 11

Chapter 6   Focus Groups 13

Chapter 7   Amazon FBA 17

Chapter 8   Amazon Kindle, Create Space, & Audible 21

Chapter 9   Dropshipping 23

Conclusion 25

Chapter 1

The Search for Passive Income

There are several forms of passive income. The easiest way to begin your search for passive income is to conduct a google search. In 2013, I began my journey to financial freedom. The first search that appeared on google search results was on-line surveys. At first I was skeptical like everyone else that I knew. If it sounds too good to be true, you should not waste your time. I decided to take a chance. All I had to do is sign up for each individual on-line survey account and I was on my way. There are over 50 strategies to generate Passive Income but I will only share 10 of them with you to help jump start you on the path to financial freedom.

Chapter 2

On-line Surveys

On-line surveys are a legitimate way to make additional income. I would not quit my full time job and rely solely on on-line surveys to pay all of your expenses. You can earn an additional $200 to $300 a month working on-line completing surveys part-time. I would complete surveys anytime and anywhere. If I'm waiting at the barbershop to get a haircut, I'm not wasting time on Facebook and Instagram, I'm actually on my cell phone completing on-line surveys that the company sends you once you sign up. They have a lot of surveys that you can complete on your mobile device, including tablets. By the time, it was time for me to get my haircut, I had completed enough on-line surveys to pay for my haircut and the tip. Now, that is impressive. I love on-line surveys because there is no limit to your earning potential. People ask me all the time, how much can you make completing on-line surveys and I reply, it depends on how much money you want to make and how much time that you are going to dedicate to completing the surveys. When I'm watching football, basketball, or anything on television, I'm completing surveys at the same time. All of the time that people waste on social media, they could be spending completing on-line surveys. Time is money and it should be used wisely. If I'm out in town or going for a ride in my car, I'm thinking that I could be completing surveys now and making money instead of wasting time. It is a good feeling to see multiple deposits to your bank account from different survey companies. Every time that I visit home, I always bring a couple of on-line survey checks with me to show my siblings to motivate them and to show them that this is real and they can do this too. All you need is a computer, smartphone, or tablet and a high speed internet connection and you can begin today. When you first get started in the on-line survey business, you will get the lower priced surveys but as you complete more and more surveys they eventually get higher and higher. I remember completing a $25 survey in 5 minutes. It all depends on the particular survey and company that you are working with at the time. I hope that I have motivated you to get started today because I have been doing this since 2013 and it is always nice to have extra income to help support your family.

Chapter 3

EBay

One of the older ways to make passive income is through eBay. I have been a member of eBay since 2012 and I was surprised to see that I have generated over $6000 in sales and I only remember selling about $2000 worth of merchandise. That is the sweet thing about making passive income, you are making money in your sleep. Even though, Amazon is killing it right now, eBay still has millions of customers and sellers every day. So it is ok to have an Amazon and eBay account. It depends on how motivated you are and how much money you want to make. I first realized my skill when I was in the Fifth grade and my teacher sent me to the Principal's office for selling pencils in class for profit. She told the principal that she had told me to stop selling pencils in class. I explained to the Principal that this was the first time that I was told about this and I also explained to the Principal that I was an A Honor Roll student and why would I create a distraction or problem in the classroom. He agreed with me and sent me back to class. It is hard for some people to get started because everyone does not have what it takes to be an entrepreneur. It may take longer than 8 hours a day, especially when you are first starting your own business. You have to be motivated and dedicated to put in the time and effort. Most people quit and go back to their 9-5 job. The only problem with that is the fact that most people dread going to their job every day. Until you step outside of your comfort zone, you will be stuck in the rat race. You can sell products from your personal storage on eBay or you can dropship the item from various suppliers in the United States and overseas. For example, I received an order the other day for a razor blade and I drop-shipped the item from China. It takes longer to ship from overseas but as long as you list the shipping time in the description and the buyer purchases your product, you are good to go. I love eBay because they use PayPal and as soon as the customer purchased the razor blade I received an e-mail from PayPal of the deposit and an e-mail from eBay letting me know that the product was sold and that it was also available for re-listing. I immediately added the shipping number to the listing so that the customer could track his order and re-listed the razor blade on my account. The company allows you to list 50 new products a month (up to 200 total). I did not want to wait until the next month to list my new products, so I paid $0.30 for each additional product over 50 for the month. The fourth quarter of each year is the best time to sell on eBay due to the holidays, so roll up your sleeves and make it happen. The only thing holding you back is you. If you have negative people around you, you need to close your circle. My circle is very small for a reason. Who you choose to associate with says a lot about who you are as a person.

Chapter 4

YouTube Channel

The third way to make passive income is by setting up your own YouTube channel. It is not hard to set up a YouTube channel and there are actual YouTube videos that will guide you step by step to help you set up your channel. There are additional videos to help you monetize your accounts so that you can get paid for your videos. You can also take advantage of AdSense, which places ads on your videos that are popular to help you generate income. One of the new changes with YouTube personal videos is the fact that you must have at least 10,000 views before you can get paid. So the more popular your videos are, the more money you will make. You will get paid off of your video's views, watch time, and advertisements. If you go into your account, it will actually show you the different countries around the world that have viewed your video. I was surprised to see that my videos were being viewed in Afghanistan. So, you never know who will be interested in your video content, you just have to get started and promote your channel through social media, friends, and word of mouth. Remember the more videos that you upload, the more money that you will make. For example, if you have 1,000 videos uploaded and each video gets 100 views per day, which would generate you approximately $100 in passive income per day. That is good money considering the minimum wage in the United States is sad. Remember this is passive income, so this extra money that you are making without having to physically do anything once the video is edited and uploaded into the system. If you have real friends they will support you and watch your videos to help support you on your journey. If you friends and family will not take the time to watch a 5 minute video to help support you, you made need to close your circle. If I had a friend with a YouTube channel and I knew that they were trying to establish themselves in the business, I would play their video every chance that I got, but that's just me.

Chapter 5

Flipping Cars

Another way to make money is to flip used cars. I started flipping cars back in 2012. I thought that I was ready but I had no idea what I was doing. I purchased a used car for $6000 and that was the beginning of the end. I tried to get the car inspected by a mechanic before I purchased it, but the owner of the used car dealership assured me that the car was in good condition and if anything happened to the car with in the first 90 days he would have me bring it in and have it fixed at the used car mechanic shop, which was attached to the used car dealership. This should have set off a lot of alarms in my head but I was focused on flipping cars and ignored all of the signs of a bad deal. Just like clockwork, the car began to give me problems in the first week after purchase. I called the Used Car Dealership Owner and explained to him that the car needed servicing and he said that he could repair it at a discounted rate at his repair facility. So it is good to do your homework first and have any car that you plan on buying checked out by a certified mechanic before spending your hard earned money. I finally was able to flip the used car at a loss of $6000. I had spent $1000 in repairs plus the purchase price of $6000 which placed me $7000 in the hole. There are some great deals out there, you just have to be careful and if the dealer will not let you get the car checked out by a certified mechanic that you pick, please move on to a different dealership to avoid the heartache that I had to go through on my first used vehicle purchase.

Chapter 6

Focus Groups

The fifth way to generate extra income is through Focus Groups. This is one of my favorites because at the end of the Focus Group, the manager hands you a $100 bill and sometimes a $100 check. When I first heard about people getting $100 to attend a 2 hour Focus Group, I was skeptical like most people. When I showed up to the office, there was a secretary at the front desk and she took my information and had me sit in the waiting area where there was lunch on standby. I was surprised to see other people there already with Harry Potter book, movies, and memorabilia. The Focus Group was on Harry Potter and they were prepared for the Focus Group questions. The hardest part in regards to being selected for a Focus Group is the initial questioning over the phone. This is where you will find out if you are eligible for the Focus Group. I remember being screened out for a $225 Focus Group because of the initial questions that the company asked you when they are filling their quotas. The other side of that, is that if they call you in for a Focus Group, you will get paid at the end of the meeting in cash or check. How many of you have been to a Police Station? Ok, then you are familiar with the interview room. When you are in a Focus Group, there are observers behind a double-sided mirror that can see you and they record and watch everything during the Focus Group. If you do not participate much during the Focus Group, they will call you out and ask you if you have any input or opinion on the topic or particular question. They have to pay you once you leave, so they want to make sure that they get their money's worth. I also remember conducting a Focus Group on Haagen-Dazs ice cream container. They went into great detail in regards to the container design in relation to customer appeal and how the particular product made you feel. You will be amazed of the depth of the various Focus Groups. Once you complete you one or two hour Focus Group, you and you fellow group members will line up and head towards the front desk where the secretary is waiting with the $100 bill or check. I was shocked to receive $100 for two hours of questioning. I always thought that opportunities like this were fiction and that the media was making all of this up to get attention until I actually did it myself. Now, Focus Groups pay a lot more than surveys but they are not easy to screen and get approved for. So, if you get the opportunity to participate in a Focus Group and you have the time, please take advantage of this unique opportunity because it pays to give your opinion.

Chapter 7

Amazon FBA

The sixth way to create passive income is through Amazon FBA or fulfillment by Amazon. This is a great way to start your own private E-Commerce business. Amazon has over 300 million active customers in their system waiting to purchase new products with the click of a button. It is real easy to get signed up for Amazon FBA. I actually used YouTube to help me sign up for the business. It was not difficult and it guided me step by step. Once your account is created, you can list as an individual and Amazon will charge you $0.99 per purchase or you can take advantage of fulfillment by Amazon, which is highly recommended, to help support your business. This particular service is $39.99 a month. It may be hard when you first start but anything worthwhile is going to involve some sacrifice. If it were easy, everybody would be doing it. Once you are signed up, you need to list your first product. I recommend a product that is small, light, and inexpensive to ship. Most of the entrepreneurs outsource from overseas and the lighter the product, the cheaper the shipping costs. If you want to sell any kind of health or supplement products, I highly recommend going through the United States due to the Food and Drug Administration and various inspections that the product must past including customs before entering the United States. Amazon allows you to sell on Amazon.com, Amazon (Canada), and Amazon (Mexico). So, the potential to earn lots of money is unlimited. A god starting point to find a profitable product is to go to amazon.com and check the best sellers list. This will give you a good idea of the product or products that you would like to begin selling online. Once you get you product listed on Amazon FBA, you will need the shipping address of the manufacturer that you are using to enter into the system. This can be time consuming, especially if your manufacturer is overseas. I remember e-mailing my first manufacturer in China and I asked for his shipping address and he replied, "Why do you need my shipping address?" His response told me three things right away. One, he was inexperienced in business, two, he was rude to a potential long-term customer, and three, I was going to look for another manufacturer. Once you get the shipping address from the manufacturer, you will need to enter it into your Amazon FBA account. Then you will continue to fill in your account information. You will have to label each of your products with a bar code so that Amazon can scan and store your products in the Fulfillment Warehouse. If you do not want to attach a bar code to each one of your products, you have the option to pay Amazon $0.20 per bar code to label the products for you. For example, if you have 100 products that you are sending to the fulfillment center, you will pay Amazon $20 to label all 100 products. When you are first starting out, it is a good idea to send the products to your house. This way you can inspect the quality of the products and print and label each product and save the $0.20 Amazon labeling fee. After you have inspected and labeled all of your products, you will need to print the UPS Shipping label (cheapest), so that you can take your product to the Post Office and mail to the Amazon Fulfillment centers on the East and West Coast. The reason that you want to mail your product to both coasts is simple. If someone orders one of your products on Amazon.com from Florida, the Amazon Fulfillment center on the East Coast will ship the product to the customer and vice versa. Once your products are at the Amazon Fulfillment centers, all you have to do is ensure that your inventory is stocked. Once an order is placed, Amazon will pack, ship, and deliver the product to the customer. They also deal with returns and customer service. So, all you need to do is sit back and monitor the deposits directly to your personal bank account.

Chapter 8

Amazon Kindle, Create Space, & Audible

The seventh, eighth, and ninth way to create Passive Income is to write your own book. Amazon Kindle offers the eBook, Create Space offers a hard copy book, and audible or ACX offers an audible version of your book. I know that this can be intimidating to anyone, but what do you have to lose? You can write on any topic that peaks your interest. I highly recommend that you visit Amazon to see what books are actually selling right now so that your book is profitable niche. Amazon Kindle makes it very easy to publish your own personal eBook. Once you sign up for Amazon Kindle Direct Publishing, they will take you step by step to help you create your first book. The hardest part is making the first step to get started and create an account. Once you get started, you will be surprised on how far you can go when you get the ball rolling. There are also a lot of

YouTube videos that will help you throughout your journey. There are two options to receive royalties with your eBook. One is 35% and the other is 70% and it has a set price range for your eBook in each category. I highly recommend that you sell your first book for $0.99 because you are new to the market and you want to get reviews and establish reviews and rankings. Once you are established, you can always go back and change the price of your book. This is just advice and you can list your book at whatever price that you feel that it is worth. I hope that you will take my advice because it will help you in the long run. If you get lost at any time, please utilize YouTube and there is a step-by-step video on how to complete the entire process.

Chapter 9

Dropshipping

The tenth way to generate massive income is dropshipping. The great thing about this strategy is the fact that you can use multiple sources as your supplier. I usually source out of China but sometimes there is an issue with the supplier, so I always have two backup sources and sometimes I will have the product at my house. You always want to have more than one supplier. This way if there is an issue with your main supplier, you have a backup and you will not lose your customer base. Once you run out of stock on Amazon, they will pull your product listing and it will show out of stock when you log into your account. So, you have to be proactive, because this is a legitimate business and you want your customers to receive their products promptly. So when your inventory is getting low, you should already be on-line or on the phone ordering more supplies to re-stock the Amazon Fulfillment Warehouse on the East and West Coast. At the same time, you are going to have to manage your finances. If you are not good at managing finances, I highly recommend that you get an Accountant. If you spend all of your money on frivolous things, you will not be able to restock your product and your product will be pulled from the product listing on Amazon and this could negatively affect your ranking on Amazon, which directly affects your sales revenue.

Conclusion

In conclusion, there are over 50 forms of passive income. We have just scratched the surface with the first ten. If you really want to earn more cash flow for you and your family, all you need to do is use your head to create positive cash flow and acquire assets. Once you acquire assets and receive more cash flow, buy more assets and you will eventually become wealthy as long as you minimize expenses and eliminate liabilities. I hope that this helps you on your journey to financial freedom.

www.ingramcontent.com/pod-product-compliance
Lightning Source LLC
Chambersburg PA
CBHW050035230526
45470CB00003B/1295